DISCARDED

PIZARRO

Great Explorers of the World

Conqueror of the Mighty Incas

Liz Sonneborn

Enslow Publishers, Inc.
40 Industrial Road
Box 398
Berkeley Heights, NJ 07922
USA
http://www.enslow.com

Library of Congress Cataloging-in-Publication Data

Sonneborn, Liz.
  Pizarro : conqueror of the mighty Incas / Liz Sonneborn.
    p. cm. — (Great explorers of the world)
  Summary: "Examines the life of Spanish explorer Francisco Pizarro, including his early explorations
in the Americas, his conquest of Peru and the Inca Empire, and his death and legacy"—Provided by
publisher.
  Includes bibliographical references and index.
  ISBN-13: 978-1-59845-128-3
  ISBN-10: 1-59845-128-6
  1. Pizarro, Francisco, ca. 1475–1541—Juvenile literature. 2. Peru—History—Conquest,
1522–1548—Juvenile literature. 3. South America—Discovery and exploration—Spanish—Juvenile
literature. 4. Governors—Peru—Biography—Juvenile literature. 5. Explorers—Peru—Biography—
Juvenile literature. 6. Explorers—South America—Biography—Juvenile literature. 7. Explorers—
Spain—Biography—Juvenile literature. I. Title.
  F3442.P776S665 2010
  985'.02092—dc22
  [B]
                                                    2009008996

Printed in the United States of America

092009 Lake Book Manufacturing, Inc., Melrose Park, IL

10 9 8 7 6 5 4 3 2 1

To Our Readers: We have done our best to make sure all Internet Addresses in this book were active
and appropriate when we went to press. However, the author and the publisher have no control over
and assume no liability for the material available on those Internet sites or on other Web sites they
may link to. Any comments or suggestions can be sent by e-mail to comments@enslow.com or to the
address on the back cover.

Enslow Publishers, Inc., is committed to printing our books on recycled paper. The paper in every
book contains 10% to 30% post-consumer waste (PCW). The cover board on the outside of each book
contains 100% PCW. Our goal is to do our part to help young people and the environment too!

Illustration Credits: © AISA / Everett Collection, pp. 1, 14, 96; The Art Archive / Biblioteca
Nazionale Marciana Venice / Gianni Dagli Orti, pp. 48–49, 55, 68–69; The Art Archive / Museo del
Oro Lima / Gianni Dagli Orti, p. 9; Biblioteca Universidad, Barcelona, Spain / The Bridgeman Art
Library, pp. 84–85; Bildarchiv Preussischer Kulturbesitz / Art Resource, NY, pp. 28–29, 34, 41;
Enslow Publishers, Inc., p. 38; The Granger Collection, New York, pp. 25, 44, 65, 82; © Jupiterimages
Corporation, pp. 12, 23, 103; Leandro Neumann Ciuffo, pp. 18–19; Library of Congress, p. 75;
© Shutterstock ®, pp. 58, 80, 104; © Topham / The Image Works, p. 90; Courtesy of the University
of Texas Libraries, The University of Texas at Austin, p. 61.

Ship Illustration Used in Chapter Openers: © Jupiterimages Corporation.

Cover Illustration: © AISA / Everett Collection (Portrait of Francisco Pizarro).

Contents

EXPLORER TIMELINE

circa 1477—Francisco Pizarro is born in Trujillo, Spain.

1492— Christopher Columbus makes his first voyage to the Americas.

circa 1496—Pizarro leaves home to join the Spanish army in Italy.

1502— Journeys to the Americas for the first time.

1513— Serves as an officer under Vasco Núñez de Balboa during his exploration of Panama.

1519— Hernán Cortés conquers the Aztecs of Mexico; the Spanish city of Panama is founded.

1524–1525—Pizarro makes his first exploration of the coast of what is now South America.

1526— *November*: Leaves Panama for his second exploration of the South American coast.

1527— *August*: Most of Pizarro's men abandon his expedition; Pizarro convinces the "glorious thirteen" to continue on.

1528— *May*: Pizarro encounters Inca Indians at the town of Tumbes.

1529— *July*: The Spanish queen, Isabella of Portugal, approves Pizarro's request to explore and conquer the Inca Empire.

1530— *December*: Pizarro leads an expedition out of Panama bound for the Inca Empire.

1532— *November*: Takes the Inca emperor Atahualpa prisoner in the town of Cajamarca.

1533— *July*: Orders the execution of Atahualpa.

— *November*: Pizarro and his men enter the Inca capital of Cuzco.

— *December*: Manco Inca is named the new emperor of the Incas.

1535— *January*: Pizarro founds Lima as the capital of Spanish-held Peru.

1536–1537—Manco Inca rebels against the Spanish and lays siege to Cuzco.

1537— *April*: Pizarro's partner Diego de Almagro takes over Cuzco.

1538— *April*: Pizarro's army, led by his brother Hernando, defeats Almagro's forces.

— *July*: Hernando Pizarro orders the execution of Almagro.

1539— *April–July*: Pizarro's brother Gonzalo unsuccessfully battles Manco Inca at his jungle stronghold of Vilcabamba.

1541–1542—Gonzalo Pizarro and Francisco de Orellana lead an expedition to the Amazon region east of Peru.

1541— *June 26*: Francisco Pizarro is murdered by supporters of Almagro.

1544— Manco Inca is killed by Almagro's followers in the Inca town of Vitcos.

1545— Silver deposits are discovered in what is now Potosí, Bolivia.

1548— *April*: Gonzalo Pizarro is executed after rebelling against Spanish authorities in Peru.

1572— *September*: Manco Inca's son Túpac Amaru is killed in Cuzco, ending Inca resistance to Spanish rule.

1578— *August*: Hernando Pizarro dies in Spain.

1590— *January*: Mansio Serra de Leguizamón, the last of Pizarro's conquistadores, dies.

Chapter 1

A Line in the Sand

In the late summer of 1527, a group of eighty men were living on an otherwise uninhabited island in the Pacific Ocean. The men were exhausted and in poor health. They had little food to eat. They had to survive on snake meat and shellfish. Their bodies were battered from days spent in the hot sun. Many had open sores on their feet and faces. Each week, a few died of disease.

For the past ten months, the men had been traveling down the western coast of South America. They were very far from home. They had come to the Americas from Spain.

They were not great explorers looking for adventure. They were instead poor men hoping to better their lives. The men were part of a great wave of Spaniards to arrive in the Americas. Ever since Christopher Columbus landed in the Americas in 1492, Spaniards had come there in search of riches.

PIZARRO'S EXPEDITION

The small group's leader was Francisco Pizarro. About fifty years old, Pizarro had arrived in the Americas as a young man.

For decades, he worked as a slaver. He enslaved and sold American Indians. It was a brutal and cruel business. But Pizarro was very successful. He had a fine home in Panama. It was a Spanish city built on the narrow strip of land that joined North and South America.

His comfortable life in Panama was not enough for Pizarro. He wanted even more wealth. With two business partners, he set out to explore the South American coast. He went in search of a fabled land where Indian peoples mined gold and silver.

If he found it, Pizarro intended to fight the Indians and steal their riches. Promising to share the treasure, he recruited about 160 desperate men to join his expedition. They had set off from Panama with two ships in November 1526.

Meeting the Incas

After sailing a short distance down the coast, the expedition split up. Pizarro's partner Diego de Almagro headed back to Panama for supplies and new recruits. Pizarro camped along the San Juan River in what is now Colombia.

Ship captain Bartolomé Ruiz took charge of a third group. His small party sailed farther south. After crossing the equator, it reached the coast of present-day Ecuador. There, Ruiz spied a large wooden raft. A group of Inca Indian traders were on board.

The Spaniards marveled at their goods. They had woven wool and cotton cloth, some embroidered with birds, animals, and trees. But even more exciting to the Spaniards than these items were their beautiful gold and silver objects. The Incas had bracelets, necklaces, mirrors, and cups made from these precious metals.

The Spaniards marveled at the gold and silver objects the Incas made. This is a gold statuette from the Inca Empire.

Ruiz took three Inca boys captive. He wanted them to act as translators. Using sign language, they told Ruiz that their trade goods came from a land to the south—a land that teemed with gold and silver.

TRYING TIMES

Ruiz returned to Pizarro's camp. Pizarro was encouraged by news of Ruiz's encounter. He and his men continued to probe the coast looking for treasure. Low on supplies, they established a camp on an island in mid-1527. They called it *Isla del Gallo,* meaning "Island of the Cock." Its shape reminded them of a cock's comb—the fleshy growth on the top of a rooster's head.

Pizarro and his men settled down in their island camp and waited for the supply ships to arrive. As time passed, the men's situation grew more and more desperate. They were starving and some were getting sick. Many began to blame Pizarro for their miserable situation. They called him a madman.

Some decided to contact the Spanish governor of Panama. Unknown to Pizarro, they wrote the governor a note. They hid it in a bale of wool Ruiz carried back to Panama. The wool was a gift for the governor's wife.

In the note, the men said Pizarro was a vicious butcher. If he had his way, they would all be dead.

They begged the governor to send a ship to take them back home.

The ship arrived in August 1527. The governor sent word that all men who wanted to leave could go. Pizarro could not force anyone to stay.

PIZARRO MAKES HIS CASE

But Pizarro would not to give up. He tried to persuade his men to remain on the island. Pizarro, usually a quiet man, struggled to find the words to change his men's minds. If he failed, it would spell the end of his expedition.

Pizarro and his men gathered on the beach. He took out his sword. With its tip, he drew a line in the sand.

While speaking, he pointed to one side of the line, and then to the other. Pizarro said, "Comrades and friends; *there* lies the part that represents death, hardship, hunger, nakedness, rains, and abandonment; this side represents comfort. Here you return to Panama to be poor; *there*, you may go on to Peru to be rich. Choose which best becomes you as good Spaniards!"[1]

THE GLORIOUS THIRTEEN

The Spanish historian Cieza de León later wrote about what happened next. To Pizarro's disappointment, not one man wanted to stay.

This mosaic from Pizarro's tomb in Lima Cathedral depicts Pizarro and his soldiers on the island of Gallo. On this island, Pizarro drew his famous line in the sand.

Pizarro then reminded them of the gold and silver Ruiz had seen. When that did not work, he talked about his dedication to their mission. As León wrote, "He took satisfaction in one thing: if they had all gone through hardships and starvation, he had shared it with them."[2]

His words finally convinced thirteen men. They later became known in Spanish history as the "glorious thirteen." The captain on the rescue ship agreed to take them and Pizarro to another island called Gorgona. He dropped them, a store of corn, and the three Indian interpreters off the coast.

CONTINUING ON

The men were stranded without a ship. But Gorgona was a little more hospitable than Gallo. At least there were turtles, lizards, and birds that the Spaniards could kill for food. Pizarro and his small band stayed there for seven months, all the while dreaming of golden lands to the south.

Finally, in March 1528, a rescue ship piloted by Ruiz reached them. Pizarro's men were relieved. But Pizarro was even more pleased. He finally had a ship to continue his expedition.

Leaving the sick behind on Gorgona to recover, Pizarro and Ruiz headed south. The farther they traveled the more Inca traders they saw. Finally, in late April, they reached the Inca town of Tumbes in present-day Peru.

Francisco Pizarro

The Incas of Tumbes

The Incas gawked at their Spanish visitors. They had never seen white men before. They could not help but stare at their peculiar bushy beards. The Incas were even more intrigued by an African servant the Spanish brought with them. They asked to watch him wash to see if the black color of his skin would come off.

These newcomers were strange. But the Incas were not afraid of them. They welcomed the Spaniards and offered them food.

Pizarro sent several of his men ashore. The Spaniards were just as astounded as the Incas by what they saw. Tumbes was a busy place, full of stone buildings and fertile fields. They were all struck by the Incas' warmth and friendliness.

Pizarro Plans His Return

Pizarro had little interest in these things. There was one detail that did impress him, however. He learned that the walls of a temple in Tumbes were covered with gold.

Pizarro soon left Tumbes and sailed back to Panama. But he resolved to return to the Incas' lands. His next expedition would change far more than the lives of Pizarro and his men. It would spell the end of the Incas' world and the beginning of the Spanish takeover of South America.

Chapter 2

A Soldier of Fortune

In about 1477, Pizarro was born in Trujillo, Spain. He probably spent his childhood there. The man that historians believe to be Pizarro's father, Gonzalo, was a hidalgo—a title bestowed on successful soldiers.[1]

Although he was not rich, Gonzalo Pizarro had a small estate. He was considered an important man in Trujillo.

Like most Spanish men of the day, Gonzalo had many children. He had three with his wife. But he had others with his mistresses. One of his mistresses was Francisca González, Pizarro's mother. She was probably a young servant in the town's convent.

Pizarro was likely welcome on his father's estate. But because he was illegitimate, his father did not fund his education. Pizarro never learned to read or write. Little is known about his early life. But by some accounts, Pizarro spent his youth tending his father's pigs.[2]

Exploring the Americas

Pizarro would not inherit anything from his father. (Everything would instead go to Gonzalo's only legitimate son,

Hernando.) Therefore, Francisco Pizarro had to find a way to make his own living. Like many ambitious but poor men, he went into the military. When he was about nineteen, he probably joined the Spanish army and traveled to Italy.

About five years later, Pizarro set off for the Americas. By then, he had become a skilled soldier. He worked under several commanders. With them, he explored areas in the Caribbean Islands and Central America. These expeditions searched for gold, and Indians to enslave. Pizarro gained a reputation for treating Indians with great cruelty.

Francisco Pizarro was born in Trujillo, Spain, in about 1477. This is the Plaza Mayor in Trujillo today.

One Spaniard who knew him said that "this evil habit was much used, and Pizarro knew it by heart, having used it for years before."[3]

In 1513, Pizarro served as a senior officer under Vasco Núñez de Balboa. He joined Balboa on his explorations of the Isthmus of Panama. Traveling through Panama's thick forests, Balboa's men reached the Pacific Ocean. They were the first Europeans to see this body of water.

After this expedition, Pizarro helped settle the Spanish city of Panama. There, he heard of a land to the south. It was supposedly full of great riches.

In 1522, explorer Pascual de Andagoya traveled down the Pacific coast in search of this land. He reached a river named Biru. The Spanish named the land a version of the river's name. They called it Peru.

ENTICED BY PERU

Andagoya became ill. He could not continue his exploration of Peru. Pizarro then decided to go in search of it himself. To help finance the expedition, he took on two partners. One was Diego de Almagro—a friend of Pizarro's. The two men had much in common. They were about the same age. They had both grown up poor. And they had both left Spain for the Americas to make their fortune.

The second partner was Hernando de Luque. Unlike Pizarro and Almagro, he was not a military man. He was a priest. His role in the partnership was probably limited to gathering funds for the expedition.

WANTING MORE

At the time, Pizarro was in his late forties. Given his humble beginnings in Trujillo, he had become surprisingly successful. Pizarro was a very wealthy and well-respected man. He had served as a city official in Panama. He also owned a large ranch there.

Why did Pizarro want to go to Peru? After all, it was a risky and expensive venture. He would be traveling far from any Spanish settlements. If he got into trouble, he would largely be on his own.

Pizarro also had no idea what he would find in Peru. Perhaps he would discover no riches. Then he might lose all the money he invested in the expedition. Perhaps he would run into hostile Indians. Then he might lose something even dearer—his life.

Pizarro lived comfortably in Panama. But that lifestyle did not suit him. His ambitious nature made him restless. He would not be happy to see anyone else reap a fortune that he could snatch himself.

CORTÉS AND THE AZTECS

Hernán Cortés and his conquest of Mexico also likely inspired Pizarro. Cortés was a cousin of Pizarro's father. In 1519, Cortés set off from Cuba with more than five hundred men. He had heard of a great civilization in the heart of what is now Mexico. With his small army, he discovered the huge empire of the Aztecs.

Montezuma, the Aztec ruler, allowed Cortés to enter his lands. He may have thought the stranger was a god. But more likely, the Aztecs were most intrigued by what the Spaniards brought with them. They rode horses. The Aztecs had never seen these animals before. They also had a cannon and guns. These weapons, too, were unknown in the Aztec world.

Cortés did not return Montezuma's friendship. Instead, he murdered the Aztec leader and took over the empire's capital. His men slaughtered countless Aztecs and destroyed their society.

Cortés was a conquistador, the Spanish word for conqueror. Through brutal warfare, he took control of the wondrous treasures of the Aztec Empire. In the process, he became an unbelievably wealthy man. Carlos I also honored Cortés. He was the king of Spain. (Carlos I was also known as Charles V—the ruler of the Holy Roman Empire.) Cortés's conquest of the Aztecs pleased Carlos I. As king, he claimed a portion of the Aztecs' wealth for himself.

Pizarro's First Peruvian Explorations

Pizarro made his first exploration of the South American coast between 1524 and 1525. With Almagro and eighty men, he traveled much the same route Andagoya had taken. The venture was a disaster. Disease or hostile Indians killed most of his men. During an Indian attack, Almagro lost one of his eyes.

Pizarro returned to Panama to plan a second voyage. But the first was so unsuccessful that very

Hernán Cortés meeting with Montezuma, leader of the Aztecs. The riches Cortés brought back to Spain greatly impressed King Carlos I.

few investors wanted to support another voyage. Nevertheless, Pizarro and his partners eventually found the money they needed. Pizarro and his soldiers set off on their second expedition in November 1526. In the beginning, the expedition looked promising. Early on, his captain Bartolomé Ruiz encountered Inca traders with stores of gold and silver.

Yet, by August 1527, Pizarro's men were sick and starving. Most of his crew abandoned him and returned to Panama. With the rugged men later known as the glorious thirteen, Pizarro continued on. He finally reached the Inca town of Tumbes. The visit there suggested that the Incas were an advanced people. It also gave Pizarro his first chance to see the Incas' riches with his own eyes— a sight he would not soon forget.

● A TRIP TO SPAIN

Pizarro's first two expeditions down the South American coast were hardly great successes. But he did learn that the rumors about Inca gold and silver were true.

Pizarro began planning a third expedition. But before heading out to Peru, he returned to Spain. His partners had encouraged him to go. They all wanted to get the king's official approval for their expedition.

Pizarro meeting with King Carlos I in 1528. Pizarro was seeking the king's approval to conquer new territories in South America, including the Inca Empire.

In late 1528, Pizarro arrived in Toledo. The city housed the court of Carlos I. Pizarro had a brief meeting with the king. He presented him with some gold items gathered during his second expedition in Peru.

Pizarro also brought exotic animals from South America. He gave the king several colorful tropical birds. He also offered King Carlos a few llamas. The Incas did not have horses, as the Spaniards did. They instead used llamas as pack animals. The king placed the llamas and tropical birds in his private zoo.

Carlos I was pleased with Pizarro's gifts. But they did not impress the king. A year before, Hernán Cortés had dazzled his court with Mexican treasures made from gold, silver, and precious gems. Pizarro's offerings from Peru seemed measly in comparison.

CONVINCING THE CROWN

The king told Pizarro to speak to the Council of the Indies. This group managed the Spanish colonies in the Americas. For months, Pizarro tried to get a meeting with the council. But the council was too busy to see him. Finally, the influential Count of Osorno took an interest in Pizarro's plans. He spoke with the Spanish queen, Isabella of Portugal. She approved Pizarro's expedition.

The Spanish government made Pizarro a knight. It also named Pizarro the sole captain of the expedition. If he succeeded in conquering Peru, he would become its governor. Pizarro would share any treasures he found with the Spanish king.[4]

The Spanish government also insisted that Pizarro recruit at least 150 men for his expedition. The crew had to include a few priests. The Spanish were Catholics, and they sent many priests to the Americas. The priests were to convert Indians to Christianity.

The conquistadores treated Indians cruelly and stole their wealth. But the Spanish were able to brush aside these moral wrongs. The Spaniards insisted they were doing God's work by bringing Christianity to American Indian peoples. In this way, the Spanish used their religion to justify their brutal conquest of the Americas.

Pizarro left Toledo and headed to Trujillo. He had not seen his hometown for many years. There, he hoped to recruit men for his expedition. Pizarro first signed up three of his young half brothers: Hernando, Juan, and Gonzalo. He had never met Juan and Gonzalo before. Pizarro had left Trujillo before they were even born. Pizarro also recruited a fifteen-year-old relative, Pedro, to serve as his personal servant. Many years later, when he was an old man, Pedro Pizarro wrote a book about his adventures in Peru.

At the right of this engraving, Pizarro, Diego de Almagro, and Hernando de Luque, discuss their agreement about the expedition to Peru.

🌐 Rounding Up Recruits

Pizarro then gathered a crowd in the town square. He explained his plans to conquer Peru. Pizarro showed the townspeople gold and precious stones from this faraway land. Pizarro acknowledged that the expedition would be difficult. He even admitted that on his last exploration, his men almost mutinied. Pizarro praised the glorious thirteen who had remained loyal to him. He wanted would-be recruits to know he valued loyalty above all else.

The crowd at Trujillo was made up of peasants. They were very poor. The lure of riches must have tempted many of the listeners. But only seventeen men agreed to join Pizarro. To the rest, the expedition sounded too difficult and dangerous.

Pizarro continued on to the Spanish port of Seville. He spent months in the city rounding up more than one hundred recruits. He also bought three ships, and the supplies he would need. They included mules, horses, and a herd of pigs.

🌐 Pizarro's Deal

In January 1530, Pizarro set sail for Panama. There, he reunited with his business partners, Almagro and Luque. When Pizarro told them about his new deal with the Spanish government, they became furious. The three partners were supposed to share in the profits from their expedition.

But the Spanish Crown had declared only Pizarro would get a share of Peru's riches. It assigned wealth found in other areas to Almagro and Luque. But the two men knew these regions were unlikely to yield as much gold as Peru.

Almagro and Luque accused Pizarro of cheating them. They refused to give him the money they had collected to fund the expedition.[5] Without these funds, Pizarro could not afford to leave Panama. His men became restless. As time went on, they were overtaken by disease and hunger. Once again, Pizarro's men were close to mutiny.

A Fragile Partnership

Pizarro met with Almagro to see if they could iron out their differences. Almagro also visited with Hernando Pizarro. Almagro told him he would provide some of Hernando's men with horses. But Almagro never made good on his promise. Hernando became very angry. As Pedro Pizarro later recalled, he "spoke very ill of [Almagro]" and called him vulgar names.[6]

Finally, Francisco Pizarro secured the ships he needed to launch the expedition. Almagro then made up with the two Pizarro brothers. He knew he would not see the profits he had hoped for. But something was better nothing. The partners were once again friends. But, as Pedro noted, there was still "much ill will on both sides."[7]

Chapter 3

The Conquistador and the Inca

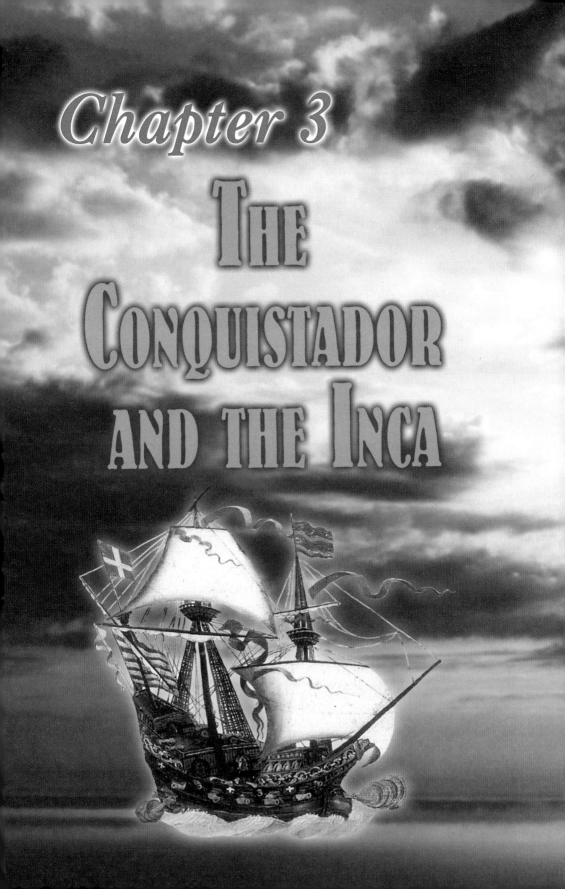

On December 27, 1530, Francisco Pizarro began his third voyage down the South American coast. In three ships, his 180 men set off for Peru. Among them were twelve of the glorious thirteen. This time, Pizarro's goal was grander. Previously, he was just looking for the land of the Incas. On this expedition, he was ready to conquer the entire empire.

His partners stayed in Panama. Pizarro charged Diego de Almagro with finding fresh recruits. Later, he would sail to Peru with them and a load of supplies. Hernando de Luque, however, would never see the land of the Incas. He would die two years later. Luque never learned what had happened to Pizarro.

THE GREAT INCA

When Pizarro set out, he knew little about the Incas. He assumed their leader had a small, but wealthy kingdom. However, their leader ruled a great empire. The Inca Empire began when a small group founded the city-state of Cuzco in the twelfth century. But the empire greatly expanded in the fifteenth century. By the time Pizarro arrived, the Incas' lands stretched over seven hundred thousand square miles. It included parts of present-day Ecuador, Peru, Bolivia, Chile, and Argentina.

The empire's leader was called the Inca. When Pizarro began his explorations, the Inca was Huayna Cápac. He was commanding and greatly respected by the Inca people. Huayna Cápac was

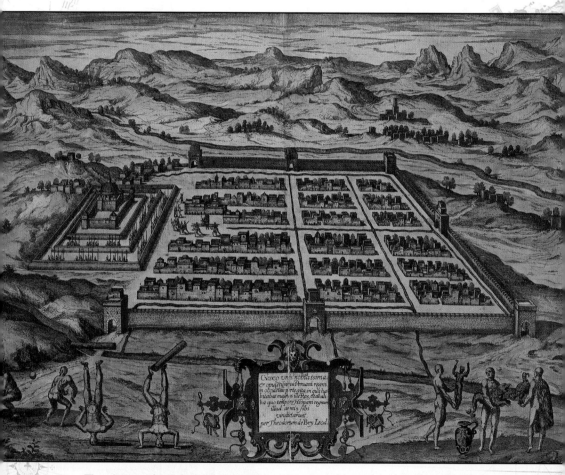

The Incas founded their empire in the city-state of Cuzco. This illustration shows Cuzco during the height of the Inca Empire in the sixteenth century.

the eleventh Inca. The Incas ruled from Cuzco, the empire's capital. It was located in what is now southeastern Peru.

During the 1400s, the Incas began fighting neighboring tribes. Through war and conquest, they took over more territory. By the 1520s, the Inca Empire included about twelve million people. Huayna Cápac believed he had conquered the entire world.

THE SON OF THE SUN

The Inca people had complex religious beliefs. Every month, they held a different religious ceremony. They worshipped many gods, including Viracocha. They believed this god created the earth, sky, and all living things.

The Incas also thought their ruler was divine. They said he was the son of the Sun.

The relatives of the Inca were revered as well. The Inca usually married his sisters. This way, the royal bloodline remained pure. Each Inca had several wives and many children.

Other relatives of the Inca were part of a class of nobles. They received wealth and other privileges. Some noblemen helped govern the regions within the empire. Others commanded the Inca's armies.

The Incas provided their ruler with goods and labor. In return, he made sure they always had

food to eat. The Inca kept great stores of food. When food was scarce, he would tap these stores to make sure no one went hungry.

BUILDING AN EMPIRE

In some ways, the Incas' world was less advanced than the Europeans'. The Incas did not know how to use a wheel. They also did not have a writing system. But in other ways, their society was very sophisticated. They loved poetry. The Incas passed down these poems by word of mouth through the generations. They also knew about astronomy and medicine.

The Incas were very skilled at cutting stone. This allowed them to construct huge and impressive stone buildings. They were so well constructed they could withstand earthquakes. The Incas knew how to build roads and bridges. Their intricate system of roads went from one end of the empire to the other. It stretched more than fourteen thousand miles. Pizarro's brother Hernando made the claim that "such magnificent roads could be seen nowhere in [Europe]."[1]

Trains of llamas walked along these roads. The Incas used these strong animals to carry goods. Messengers also ran up and down the narrow trails. These runners helped the Inca stay in contact with all of his subjects.

SMALLPOX SPREADS

In the late 1520s, the Incas suffered a major crisis. People in the northern reaches of the empire were falling ill. Many died of a strange new illness. They were victims of smallpox. Spaniards to the north spread this disease to the Incas. Smallpox was unknown in the Americas before the Spanish arrived. As a result, the Incas had no natural immunities to it.

Huayna Cápac was upset by news of the epidemic. He was responsible for the welfare of his people. To help cure them, he refused to eat. He also ordered the execution of thousands of children. He hoped these sacrifices would please Viracocha. His efforts did nothing to stop the spread of the disease.

In fact, Huayna Cápac soon became sick. He died about 1527, probably from smallpox. His body was sent to Cuzco. It was placed in a special palace. Almost one thousand of his servants were killed. The Incas believed they would serve Huayna Cápac in the afterlife.

THE INCA CIVIL WAR

The new Inca was selected from the old Inca's sons. The Villaoma was responsible for choosing which one. He was a priest of the sun.

The Villaoma first picked Ninan Cuyochi. But he died only a few days after he was picked. The

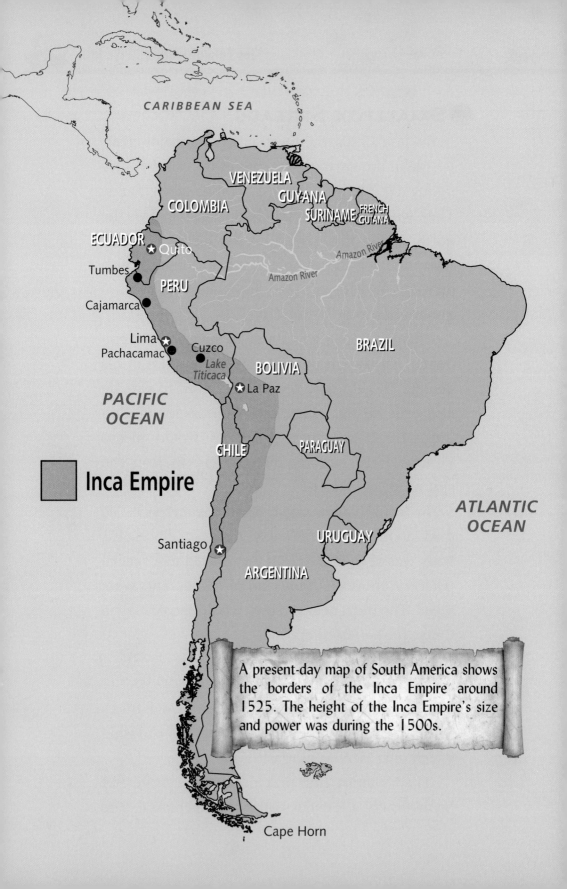

CARIBBEAN SEA

VENEZUELA

COLOMBIA

GUYANA

SURINAME

FRENCH GUIANA

ECUADOR

★ Quito

Tumbes

PERU

Cajamarca

Amazon River

Amazon River

BRAZIL

Lima ★
Pachacamac

Cuzco

Lake Titicaca

BOLIVIA

La Paz ★

PACIFIC OCEAN

CHILE

PARAGUAY

ATLANTIC OCEAN

Inca Empire

URUGUAY

Santiago ★

ARGENTINA

A present-day map of South America shows the borders of the Inca Empire around 1525. The height of the Inca Empire's size and power was during the 1500s.

Cape Horn

Villaoma then chose Huascar as the next Inca. Huascar was only twenty-two years old. But he was well liked by the nobles in Cuzco.

His older brother, Atahualpa, was not pleased with the decision. He wanted to be the Inca. He had assembled an army. Atahualpa decided to take over by force. Suddenly, the Incas were plunged into a violent civil war.

CAMPING IN ECUADOR

Knowing nothing of the Inca epidemic or civil war, Pizarro began his third trek down the South American coast. He soon reached what is now northern Ecuador. On shore, the men set up camp. They stayed there for seven months, waiting for the winter rains to end. Many of his men grew impatient. They wanted to reach the golden land of the Incas as soon as possible.

While they were at this camp, two Spanish ships arrived. The ships were commanded by Hernando de Soto, who brought one hundred more recruits.

In Panama, Pizarro had asked for de Soto's help. In exchange, he promised to give de Soto command of his army. But when de Soto showed up, Pizarro went back on his word. He wanted his brother Hernando to have that position.

In the spring, the Spaniards slowly began moving down the coast. Along the way, they met some Incas. The captives taken during Pizarro's second expedition helped them communicate with the Indians.

By April, the Spaniards reached Tumbes. Only four years earlier, on his second expedition, Pizarro had found Tumbes a vibrant Inca town. This time, it was completely abandoned. Its mud huts were filled with corpses. The civil war had taken a great toll on the people of Tumbes.

The gruesome discovery upset Pizarro's men. Already edgy, they came upon some large bones. They had heard wild tales from the Incas of great giants that walked among them. The Spaniards were terrified they had found the remains of these fabled beings. Frightened in this strange land, some began to wonder about Pizarro's leadership. A few even questioned his sanity.

Pizarro saw his men's anxiety. Outside Tumbes, they captured some local Inca chiefs. Pizarro had them executed as his men watched. The brutal act sent a message. The Spaniards could expect the same treatment if they tried to defy Pizarro.[2]

MONITORING THE ENEMY

The men continued their journey south. As they marched, Atahualpa carefully monitored their slow advance. His messengers told him about the light-skinned, bearded strangers. The messengers assured Atahualpa that they were not gods. They

ATAHUALLPA, INCA XIIII.

Atahualpa paid close attention to Pizarro's advance into his lands.

were just men. Atahualpa could fight and kill them if he wanted to.

At the time, Atahualpa was still fighting the war with his brother. He thought about attacking the Spaniards. But their small force did not seem like a huge threat. Instead, he concentrated on his struggle with Huascar for the Inca throne.

From local Indians, Pizarro also kept tabs on Atahualpa. They told him Atahualpa was nearby. The new Inca was in the mountain town of Cajamarca. They also told Pizarro about Atahualpa's war with his brother. This news pleased Pizarro. He saw an opportunity in the division within the Incas. In fact, some chiefs had already approached Pizarro. They were allies of Huascar. They were willing to join forces with the Spaniards in going to battle against Atahualpa.

To Cajamarca

On November 8, Pizarro's army began to ascend the Andes Mountains. Pizarro decided to confront Atahualpa at Cajamarca. The town was not a permanent settlement. It was used only occasionally by the Incas. They held ceremonies and certain government functions there.

The trek to Cajamarca was hard. High in the mountains, the air was thin. Many of the Spaniards became dizzy. It was also cold. Their hands and feet felt frozen as they traveled along the narrow trail.

Their nerves were also getting the better of them. Each step brought them closer to Atahualpa. The Spaniards knew he was ruthless in war. Pizarro told them to stay calm. "It is not appropriate to show fear," he said, "and still less to think about turning back."[3]

After a grueling weeklong hike, they finally got their first look at Cajamarca. All around the town, they saw Inca campsites. A Spanish soldier named Juan Ruiz de Arce later described the scene: "The Indians' camp looked like a very beautiful city. . . . So many tents were visible that we were truly filled with great apprehension. We never thought that Indians could maintain such a proud estate nor have so many tents in such good order."[4] The Spaniards guessed they would be facing thousands of Incas as they entered Cajamarca.

VISITING ATAHUALPA

Atahualpa had been staying just south of the town. The area was known for its natural hot springs. Atahualpa made no move to greet the strangers. He had decided to wait for the Spaniards to come to him.

Learning of Atahualpa's whereabouts, Pizarro sent several men to meet him. They found him bathing in the springs. Beautiful female servants

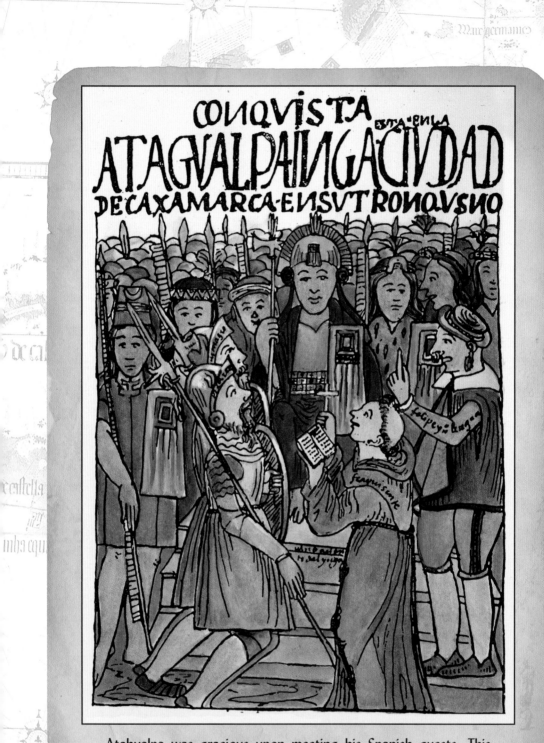

CONQVISTA ESTA ENLA
ATAGVALPAINGACIVDAD
DE CAXAMARCA-ENSVTRONOVSNO

Atahualpa was gracious upon meeting his Spanish guests. This drawing from about 1600 shows Atahualpa (center) with Pizarro kneeling at his left.

surrounded him. The Spaniards watched them snap up any stray hair that fell from Atahualpa's head. The women then ate the hairs "so that no one could use them to bewitch him."[5]

Atahualpa was a very impressive figure. One Spaniard later described his regal and powerful appearance: "Atahualpa was a man of some thirty years of age, of fine appearance and disposition, somewhat stocky, his face imposing, beautiful and ferocious."[6]

Atahualpa was gracious to his Spanish guests. He offered them golden cups filled with *chicha*. Chicha was a beer made from corn. Atahualpa's men stared at the odd visitors. They had never seen white men like this before. But they were even more fascinated by their horses. When one horse bucked, raising its front legs, a few Inca men screamed and ran away. Atahualpa later executed them for their cowardice. Atahualpa refused to be seen as weak in the eyes of his new visitors.

At one point, Hernando de Soto tried to rattle the ruler. He rode his horse close to Atahualpa. The animal's nose touched the Inca's headdress. Atahualpa, however, remained perfectly calm. He told the Spaniards they could stay the night in the empty buildings at Cajamarca. He would visit them there the following day. At that time, Atahualpa said, "I will order what shall be done."[7]

🌑 Preparing for Battle

The next morning, Pizarro carefully prepared for the Inca's arrival. At the center of Cajamarca was a great plaza. Low buildings lined three sides. On the fourth side was a wall, separating the plaza from an open field. Pizarro stationed his horsemen in the buildings. He also hid his cannon gunner and musketeers from view. Pizarro told them to wait for his signal. They were then to rush out and battle the Incas.

To the Spaniards, Pizarro's bold plan sounded insane. Their force was tiny. How could it possibly take on Atahualpa's great army? Pedro Pizarro wrote that they were "full of fear" during the long wait. He added, "I saw many Spaniards urinate without noticing it, out of pure terror."[8]

In the early afternoon, they spied Atahualpa and his followers. Hundreds of Incas marched toward the town. They wore great headdresses made of gold and silver. Their voices chanted in unison. Behind them was Atahualpa. He was seated on a litter. Eight attendants carried this heavy, silver platform on their shoulders. The Inca wore a crown and a collar made of emeralds around his neck.

Still on the litter, Atahualpa entered the plaza. Thousands of his followers also crammed into the empty town square. They were all curious to catch a glimpse of the Spaniards.

⚫ A Surprise Attack

Vicente de Valverde came forward. He was a priest. He held a wooden cross and a Bible in his hands. Through an interpreter, Valverde greeted Atahualpa. He said he came to Peru on the orders of the Spanish king. He also represented the pope. The pope was the head of the Catholic Church. Valverde told Atahualpa that he must embrace the Christian God.

Atahualpa dismissed Valverde's demands. He said he would not renounce the Incas' gods. The priest held out the Bible to him. Atahualpa made a show of flipping through the pages. Of course, the words inside meant nothing to him because he could not read them. With contempt, he threw the book on the ground.

Pizarro then signaled his men. The sound of cannon and musket fire suddenly filled the air. Spanish horsemen and foot soldiers ran into the plaza. All drew their swords and knives. Without mercy, they attacked the unarmed Incas.

In moments, the plaza was in chaos. The Spaniards slaughtered every Inca they could. The Incas panicked. They all struggled to get away. Some fell down and were trampled to death.

An Inca named Waman Pomo later wrote about the terrible scene: "They killed the Indians like ants. At the sound of the explosions and the jingle of bells on the horses' hooves, the shock of arms

The Spaniards soundly defeated the mostly unarmed Incas at Cajamarca. Atahualpa (center on his litter) was taken prisoner as Pizarro and his men continued to slaughter the Incas.

and the whole amazing novelty of their attackers' appearance, the Indians were terror stricken. . . . So many Indians were killed it was impracticable to count them."[9]

Pizarro rushed toward Atahualpa's litter. He grabbed the Inca's arm, trying to pull him off. Pizarro's men attacked the Incas holding the platform. The Spaniards hacked off their arms to make them drop the litter.

Finally, a team of horsemen grabbed the litter. They turned it on its side. Atahualpa fell to the ground. On Pizarro's orders, the great ruler was placed in chains. The Incas were shocked to see Atahualpa's capture. As one Inca witness asked, "What wonder was it, what wonder that our countrymen lost their wits, seeing blood run like water, and the Inca, whose person we all of us adore, seized and carried off by a handful of men?"[10]

The killing spree went on. For the next two hours, the Spaniards continued their attack. They murdered as many as seven thousand defenseless Indians. Before they were through, they ransacked the nearby Inca camps.

An Astounding Victory

That night, the Spaniards returned to Cajamarca. In their arms, they carried their stolen booty. The soldiers had found unbelievable treasures. They had golden cups, silver vessels, and handfuls of precious jewels.

The Spanish soldiers screamed and hooted. Pizarro shot a gun into the sky. The noise stunned the crazed men into silence.

When everyone was quiet, Pizarro said they owed their triumph to God. Pizarro believed that God had rewarded them for all the hardships they had suffered.[11]

Pizarro's men agreed. Only God could have granted them such an unlikely victory. Just hours before, they were convinced they would not survive the day. By the end of the day, they were the conquerors of the mighty Incas. And soon they would be rich beyond their wildest dreams.

Chapter 4
Exploiting the Incas

The Incas were shocked by what happened at Cajamarca. The mass murder left them terrified. But they were even more shaken by seeing Atahualpa led away in chains, begging for his life. They considered Atahualpa a god. The Incas were shocked that a few dozen strangers could overpower their great leader.

Atahualpa, too, was stunned. He had underestimated the Spaniards. He thought his army would have no trouble getting rid of these weak men. But Atahualpa did not know about their weapons. He had never seen a cannon or a steel sword. His people had not been armed at Cajamarca. But even if they had been, that would not have helped them much. Their battle-axes were no match for European weapons.

A Golden Ransom

Despite this fatal error in judgment, Atahualpa was a clever man. He quickly sized up the Spaniards. They seemed to want only one thing—treasure. Atahualpa knew at once how to deal for his freedom.

Atahualpa made his captors an offer. He proposed to pay them a ransom. This was not uncommon in the Incas' culture.

Captured war chiefs often paid ransoms to their enemies. But Atahualpa offered a ransom unlike any the Incas had ever seen. He was held in a room measuring about twenty by fifteen feet. He told the Spaniards he would fill the room with gold. By some accounts, he also promised to fill a hut with silver two times over. Once the ransom was paid, the Spaniards would set him free.[1]

Pizarro agreed to the deal. He even set it down in writing. The document promised to let Atahualpa go, as long as he did not commit treason against the Spanish.

Atahualpa sent messengers to every corner of his empire. They commanded the Incas to collect the great ransom. They also instructed the Incas to allow the Spanish soldiers to travel wherever they wanted.

ENEMIES BECOME FRIENDS

Once the deal was made, the Spaniards moved Atahualpa to larger quarters. It even had a small courtyard. Freed of his chains, Atahualpa spent his days under a kind of house arrest.

Pizarro tried to make Atahualpa comfortable. He let noble women into his quarters to serve their ruler. The Spaniards noticed that the women preserved anything he touched. They even saved old animal bones and corncobs. The women refused just to throw them away. Instead, they burned

Atahualpa (seated at left) offers Pizarro (center) a ransom in exchange for his freedom. As part of the ransom, Atahualpa promised to fill an entire room with gold.

these objects because they had been held by the son of the Sun.[2]

The Spaniards also took noble Inca women as their mistresses and wives. In appreciation for his treatment, Atahualpa gave one of his sisters to Pizarro. She was probably a young teenager at the time. Pizarro nicknamed her Pizpita after a Spanish bird. Known as Doña Inés to the Spanish, she bore Pizarro two children, a daughter and a son.

(Pizarro later married one of Atahualpa's wives, Doña Angelina. He had two children with her as well.)

Pizarro visited Atahualpa almost every day. They often ate meals together. Hernando Pizarro also became friendly with the Inca. Atahualpa admired Hernando's ability to read and write. From his guests, Atahualpa learned to speak some Spanish. They also taught him how to play card games and chess.

Atahualpa had a cup made from a human skull. Pizarro once asked him where it came from. The Inca explained that one of his brothers had once threatened him. He claimed he would kill Atahualpa. He would then drink chicha from his skull. Instead, Atahualpa killed him first. After telling the story, the Inca calmly drank beer from his brother's skull.

THE DEATH OF HUASCAR

Pizarro matched Atahualpa's brutality. He told Atahualpa to send out orders to kill many members of the royal family.[3]

They included Huascar, Atahualpa's brother and enemy. Atahualpa's followers captured Huascar and put him in a wooden cage. They made him watch as they murdered his friends and wives. Finally, they killed Huascar himself.

Pizarro's orders were shrewd. The murders were disturbing to the Inca people. The Incas were so shaken that they could not think about resisting Pizarro and his Spanish soldiers. As one Inca later explained, "[O]ur Indians lost all sense of direction. They forgot their gods and missed the authority of their rulers."[4]

Huascar's supporters were outraged by his death. It stoked their already deep hatred of Atahualpa. This was very good news for Pizarro. Atahualpa's men might try to attack the Spaniards to free their leader. If they did, he could rely on Huascar's followers for military help.[5]

Pizarro was right to fear an attack. The Inca army numbered about one hundred thousand warriors. Pizarro was holding Cajamarca with a force of only 150. The Spaniards constantly feared for their lives. At any minute, the Incas might unite and slaughter them all. Pizarro's partner Almagro was bringing reinforcements. But they would not arrive for months. Pizarro and his men could do nothing but wait. They hoped they could get their treasure before the Incas could organize a revolt.

● THIRST FOR TREASURE

Carried by trains of llama, Atahualpa's ransom trickled into Cajamarca. But by December 1532, Hernando Pizarro had grown impatient. He set off with a small expedition. They traveled a few hundred miles across the Andes Mountains. Finally, they arrived at the sacred site of Pachacamac.

Hernando's men stripped all the nearby temples of their riches. One Inca later recounted the looting. He said the Spaniards found "gold and silver vessels, jugs, pitchers, images of the puma and of foxes, or men and women, of maize [corn], of frogs and snakes."[6] The Spaniards melted down these precious objects. They produced seven tons of gold and thirteen tons of silver.

Ruins of the Inca Temple of the Sun in Pachacamac. Hernando Pizarro stripped the sacred site of all its riches, melting precious gold and silver objects into ingots.

The Incas were baffled by this practice. They were master metalworkers. They prided themselves on their incredible vessels and sculptures. To them, these objects were valuable because they were so beautiful. In contrast, the Spaniards saw gold and silver only as currency. Melting down the Inca art treasures, therefore, made perfect sense. The Incas' cups and figures were unwieldy. It was far easier to carry the metal in uniformly shaped ingots (bars). As a result, the Spaniards destroyed many spectacular Inca artworks.

● ALMAGRO ARRIVES

In the spring of 1533, on Easter Sunday, Diego de Almagro finally arrived in Cajamarca. He brought supplies and about 150 new recruits with him. Pizarro and his men were delighted. As one Spaniard later recalled, Pizarro "was greatly overjoyed by our arrival. . . . [H]e had great need of our assistance because of . . . the threat from the multitude of [Atahualpa's] warriors."[7]

Almagro was amazed at the treasures flooding into Cajamarca. But the sight of them also made him furious. Because of Pizarro's deal with the Spanish king, Almagro had no claim to the fabulous riches.

Almagro complained about the situation. Pizarro then offered him and his men a small amount of gold. Pizarro could not afford to have

Almagro too angry with him. If the Incas revolted, he would need the help of Almagro and his men. He had to keep Almagro happy.

Still, Almagro continued to grumble. The bickering between the two Spanish leaders delighted Atahualpa. It made his enemies look weak. Atahualpa also liked to make fun of Almagro. He called him "one-eyed."[8]

SHOWING OFF INCA RICHES

Pizarro was afraid Almagro might challenge his right to the ransom. He decided to send his brother Hernando back to Spain. He was to make sure King Carlos I remembered and honored Pizarro's earlier agreement.

Hernando brought crates of Inca treasures with him. It took laborers a day to unload them when Hernando reached Spain. They were put on public display. One of the most spectacular items was a life-sized statue of a boy made of solid gold.

The riches of Peru awed the Spanish people. It was clear that Pizarro had discovered a world of wealth as great as Cortés's Mexico.

A RANSOM PAID

A few days after Hernando Pizarro left for Spain, a group of Spaniards returned to Cajamarca. They had been sent to Cuzco. They reported to Pizarro that the Inca capital was filled with riches.

This map shows the path of Pizarro's conquest of Peru from 1531 to 1533. Pizarro's path is indicated by an orange line.

The men had grabbed what they could. Their booty included huge sheets of gold. These had lined the walls of a great temple. Cuzco seemed to be a treasure trove, just waiting to be looted.

By summer, the Incas had paid Atahualpa's ransom. Atahualpa expected to be set free. He thought the Spaniards were fortune hunters. After they had received their ransom, he assumed they would let him go and leave his lands.

But Atahualpa was wrong. Pizarro wanted more than the treasures brought to Cajamarca. The riches of Pachacamac and Cuzco had whetted his appetite. Pizarro did not intend on leaving the Inca Empire yet. He wanted every morsel of gold he could find.

Pizarro also had to keep Huascar's warriors happy. He would need their help if Atahualpa's army attacked. Therefore, Pizarro would do whatever the warriors' wanted to stay on their good side. And they desired one thing above all else. They wanted to see Atahualpa dead.

ACCUSING ATAHUALPA

Pizarro had promised to free Atahualpa. But, aside from the ransom, his freedom came with one condition. Atahualpa could not commit treason against the Spanish. Conveniently, Pizarro found an Inca named Felipillo willing to accuse Atahualpa of that crime. He was an Indian interpreter. Felipillo claimed he overheard Atahualpa plotting an attack on the Spaniards.

By one account, Felipillo had a good reason for making up this charge. Atahualpa had caught him sexually assaulting Atahualpa's favorite wife. Felipillo was terrified of what Atahualpa might do to him. To save himself from the Inca's wrath, Felipillo would have said anything.[9] (Almagro later accused Felipillo of conspiring against the Spanish and ordered his execution.)

Pizarro put together a hasty show trial. He accused Atahualpa of treason. The Inca was quickly found guilty. Pizarro handed down the sentence. Atahualpa would be burned at the stake. The Inca ruler was outraged. He asked Pizarro, "What have I done, or my children, that I should meet such a fate? And from your hands, too, you who have met with friendship and kindness from my people, with whom I have shared my treasures, who have received nothing but benefits from my hands!"[10]

The sentence horrified the Incas. In the past, the Incas mummified their rulers' corpses. Each mummy was then housed in its own special palace in Cuzco. On ceremonial occasions, they placed the mummies on elaborate litters and paraded them around the capital city.

The Inca people had an important reason for preserving their leaders' bodies. They believed it would ensure they would live on after death. To burn Atahualpa would not just destroy his body. It would also deny him an eternal afterlife.

On July 26, 1533, the Spaniards marched Atahualpa into the town square. As a trumpet blew, they tied him to a stake. Valverde, the priest, approached the condemned man. He offered Atahualpa a deal. The Spanish wanted Atahualpa to be baptized. In exchange, Atahualpa would be strangled rather than burned to death. Atahualpa agreed. Valverde gave him the Christian name Francisco in honor of Pizarro.

The executioners tied a rope around Atahualpa's neck. His followers cried out in sorrow. The Spaniards then twisted the rope. Soon, the Inca could no longer breathe. His body went limp. The mighty Atahualpa, the son of the Sun, was dead.

MOURNING ATAHUALPA

Pizarro's page Pedro later recalled the Incas' reaction. He said that "two of his sister-wives led the wailing for his death, singing and weeping, and recalling his great deeds."[11] The Spaniards allowed them to enter Atahualpa's quarters. There, they searched everywhere for his spirit.

According to Pedro, Pizarro grieved deeply over Atahualpa's death. He claimed, "I saw the Governor [Pizarro] weep from sorrow at being unable to grant him life."[12] Perhaps Pizarro did

Atahualpa tied to a stake before his execution. In Atahualpa's final moments, he agreed to be baptized. In exchange, the Spaniards strangled him so that he could be mummified like other Inca leaders.

feel badly about the execution. But maybe Pedro wanted to make his kinsman seem more sympathetic. Despite his efforts, Pizarro's murder of Atahualpa is still thought of as one of the worst betrayals in history.

Carlos I certainly thought Pizarro was in the wrong. He was very angry that Pizarro had killed Atahualpa without his permission. Being a king himself, Carlos I also was disturbed that the Incas' king was slaughtered so brutally. The king wrote to Pizarro: "We have been displeased by the death of Atahualpa, since he was a monarch and particularly as it was done in the name of justice."[13]

On to Cuzco

Weeks after Atahualpa's death, Pizarro left Cajamarca. He and his men headed south toward Cuzco. They hoped to find more riches there.

During the eight-hundred-mile march, the Spaniards fought four battles with the Incas. The Incas wanted to avenge Atahualpa's murder. But their campaign against the Spaniards was too disorganized. Also, their weapons were no match for guns and swords. The Inca warriors managed to kill only one Spaniard for every one hundred men they lost. They slowed down Pizarro's men, but the Inca warriors could not stop the Spanish advance.

On November 15, 1533, Pizarro's men caught their first glimpse of Cuzco. It was as large as any city they had seen in Europe. At midday, the Spaniards reached the city's center square. Great stone palaces built in honor of past Incas surrounded it. Indians fleeing the Spanish invaders had set several ablaze.

Yet, some Inca nobles at Cuzco were happy to see Pizarro. They had opposed Atahualpa's rule. They thought Atahualpa was a ruthless man who had not deserved the title the Inca. In their eyes, Pizarro was a savior.

Pizarro needed to maintain their support. He knew they wanted a new Inca. Pizarro's first choice for the job was a man named Tupac Huallpa. But a few months later, he died. Angry Incas may have poisoned him.[14]

Once in Cuzco, Pizarro named Manco Inca as the new emperor. Manco was the son of Huayna Cápac and the half brother of Atahualpa. He was only sixteen. Manco Inca became the emperor during a ceremony arranged by Pizarro. At the end, Manco Inca knelt before Pizarro. The gesture sent a message. Pizarro expected Manco Inca to do as he was told.

Looting Cuzco

Soon, the Spaniards began looting Cuzco. They stripped the temples and palaces of everything.

Their thirst for treasure stunned the Incas. Manco Inca said, "Even if all the snow in the Andes turned to gold, still they would not be satisfied."[15]

Sadly, the Inca nobles watched the Spaniards melt down their most precious possessions. They turned beautiful jewelry, cups, and statues into bars of silver and gold. The Incas were also appalled by the strangers' behavior. When they were not searching for more gold, they were getting drunk or assaulting Inca women.

The Inca nobles could do nothing to stop them. Neither could Manco Inca. He was the Inca in name only. He had no authority over the Spaniards. Pizarro, not Manco Inca, was in charge.

SETTLING PERU

Pizarro began distributing the wealth of Cuzco among his men. They each received a share of the gold and silver. Eighty men also received an *encomienda*. Each encomienda was a specific region. A man who received one was called an *encomendero*. He had control over the Incas living in his encomienda.

These Incas worked almost as slaves. They had to give their encomendero gifts of gold, food, and

During Pizarro's eight-hundred-mile march to Cuzco, his army had to fight off several Inca attacks. This 1602 engraving depicts the Spaniards in battle outside the city walls of Cuzco.

livestock. Most of Pizarro's men who received an encomienda got only one. But Pizarro and his brothers received several, making them even richer.

Some Incas had assumed the Spaniards just wanted treasure. The Incas thought the Spanish would leave with their ingots. But Pizarro had no

intention of going. By awarding the encomiendas, he showed he wanted to stay and rule Peru.

With this in mind, Pizarro founded a new city. He called it Ciudad de los Reyes. This means "city of the kings" in Spanish. The city later became known as Lima.

Lima was the new capital of Spanish-held Peru. It was located on the Pacific coast. From Lima, the Spanish sent ships back to Spain loaded with valuable booty.

When Lima was founded, Pizarro was about fifty-eight years old. He was no longer young and strong. He was an older man with a creaky body. Not surprisingly, Pizarro wanted a quieter life. He began to spend most of his time in Lima. Pizarro delighted in planning the city. He designed the plaza and the layout of the streets.

Pizarro did not have very extravagant tastes. Although he craved riches, he dressed and ate modestly. He did, however, enjoy building himself a large, luxurious house. It was the finest house in Lima. It had two patios, a stable, and a garden. Nearby he had his servants plant orchards of olive and orange trees imported from Spain.

BRIBING ALVARADO

Pizarro probably would have liked to live out his last years in Lima. But his hold on Peru remained in constant danger. One source of trouble was

Pedro de Alvarado, who was a very experienced conquistador. He had served under Hernán Cortés. Alvarado heard about the wealth found in Peru. He was determined to get his own piece of it.

Alvarado sailed to Panama with eleven ships. He brought about six hundred Spanish soldiers with him. His army was three times the size of Pizarro's. He and his men captured several ships full of supplies meant for Pizarro's men. Alvarado's intentions were clear. He wanted to take control over Peru and wrestle its riches from Pizarro.

Alvarado arrived in the Inca town of Quito. There, he met with Pizarro's partner Almagro. Almagro made him an offer. He asked Alvarado to surrender the supplies and disband his army. In return, Alvarado would receive a hefty stash of gold. Alvarado took the bribe.

Pizarro was indebted to Almagro for this clever ploy. At least for the time being, it allowed Pizarro to keep his hold over Peru.

Chapter 5

Spaniard Against Spaniard

In early 1535, Pizarro faced another challenge to his control over the Inca world. News came from King Carlos I. He declared Pizarro the commander of northern Peru and Almagro the ruler of southern Peru.

The boundary between the two areas was unclear. But Almagro was sure of one thing. He insisted that he ruled the city filled with riches, Cuzco.

JUAN AND GONZALO

Cuzco was already in a state of disarray. Pizarro had left his brothers Juan and Gonzalo in charge. They had let their followers run wild. The Spaniards continued their nonstop looting spree. Even worse, they were harassing the Inca nobles. The Spaniards demanded they reveal new stores of treasures. If they did not, the Pizarro brothers threatened to torture them all.

The Pizarros also showed contempt for Manco Inca. They publicly insulted him in front of other Incas. Manco Inca began losing the respect of his people.

Almagro decided to take over Cuzco. He arrived in the city with five hundred soldiers. They included the remnants of Pedro de Alvarado's army.

Juan and Gonzalo Pizarro were angry. They refused to recognize his authority. The brothers openly mocked Almagro. Juan even threatened to kill Hernando de Soto when he decided to take Almagro's side.

Their brother Francisco was also furious. He refused simply to let Almagro take the Inca capital. He declared, "I would rather die than surrender and abandon what I have conquered and won by my own endeavor."[1]

AN EXPEDITION TO CHILE

By May 1535, Francisco Pizarro arrived in Cuzco to take charge. The two Spanish factions were close to war. But Pizarro played his hand shrewdly. He reminded Almagro about rumors of gold in present-day Chile. The king had clearly designated this area as Almagro's territory.

Pizarro offered to help fund an expedition to Chile. He gave Almagro gold and weapons. Pizarro acted as though he wanted to help his old friend. Actually, he wanted to get Almagro out of Cuzco.

The ploy worked. That summer, Almagro led his men in search of Chilean gold. Manco Inca provided Almagro with twelve thousand Inca warriors to accompany them.

In May 1535, Pizarro arrived in Cuzco to take control of the city. In order to avoid a war, he offered to fund an expedition for Almagro to go to Chile. Here, Pizarro and Almagro swear a peace.

The confrontation over Cuzco ended Hernando de Soto's career in Peru. Pizarro no longer trusted him because of his support of Almagro. De Soto tried to join the expedition to Chile. But Almagro refused to let him. Bitter, de Soto returned to Spain. A few years later, though, de Soto came back to the Americas. He headed an expedition throughout what is now the southeastern United States. He and his men were the first Europeans to see the Mississippi River.

De Soto's adventures ended there. He fell ill and died of disease. His men buried his body in the deep Mississippi.

TORTURING MANCO INCA

Pizarro restored order in Cuzco. Then, he went back to Lima. When Hernando Pizarro returned from Spain, he was to rule the city. Meanwhile, Pizarro left his brother Juan in charge.

This proved to be a very bad decision. Juan and Gonzalo continued to abuse the Incas. Finally, Manco Inca decided he could no longer tolerate it. He plotted to wage war against the Spaniards.

At the end of 1535, Manco Inca escaped from Cuzco. He tried to raise an army to attack the Spanish invaders. But the Pizarros' men soon caught the Inca. They led him back to Cuzco as a prisoner.

The Pizarros had Manco Inca tortured. One Spaniard recalled "his guards urinated and spat in his face, stealing his clothes and belongings."[2] They also "threaten[ed] to burn him alive."[3] Manco Inca was miserable. "Why . . . if I am neither a dog nor some other such creature, do you treat me like this?" he cried.[4] Manco Inca begged his captors to strangle him. If they did not, he said, he would strangle himself. Gonzalo continued to humiliate Manco Inca even further.

HERNANDO PIZARRO RETURNS

Hernando Pizarro returned from Spain and took command of Cuzco. But little changed for the Incas. Hernando continued to torture Manco Inca. The abuse stopped only when the Inca gave him a large amount of gold and silver.

In April 1536, Manco Inca asked permission to leave Cuzco. He claimed he wanted to oversee a ceremony. After that, Manco Inca promised he would return. But he would not come back empty-handed. Manco Inca swore he would bring back to Hernando a life-size gold statue of Huayna Cápac that he had hidden.

Manco Inca's description of the statue was too much for Hernando to resist. He was desperate to get his hands on it. Greed took over his better judgment. He agreed to let Manco Inca leave the capital.

THE INCA REBELLION

Manco Inca, of course, had no intention of making good on his promise. He despised the Spaniards and the Pizarros, as did many Incas of Cuzco. Manco Inca met with his chiefs and rallied them to rebel. He said, "[W]e should attempt with every determination either to die or to kill these cruel enemies."[5]

The chiefs agreed. They knew the Spaniards had better weapons. But they felt they had no choice left but to fight. At Manco Inca's urging, they secretly sent messengers across the Inca Empire. The messengers told the Incas to come to Cuzco to do battle with the hated intruders.

At the beginning of May, Manco Inca's army was ready. Estimates of the army's size differ. But it probably included at least one hundred thousand warriors. When they descended on Cuzco, the Spaniards were terrified. They holed up into one of the city's palaces. Their force included only about 170 men.

THE SIEGE OF CUZCO

The Incas lay siege to the city. They kept all food and supplies from reaching the Spaniards inside. Soon, the Spaniards were facing certain death by starvation or disease.

In Lima, Pizarro learned about the rebellion. He was angry with his brothers for stirring up the

Incas. Now all his men in Cuzco might be killed. Pizarro's hold on Peru was hanging by a thread.

Pizarro sent three separate forces to help the trapped Spaniards. The Incas overtook each group before they reached Cuzco. Some three hundred Spaniards lost their lives in these attacks. The surviving Spaniards in Peru were panicked. Some tried to flee to Panama. But Pizarro threatened to execute any Spanish deserters.

TAKING SACSAYHUAMAN

Manco Inca organized his army from a stone fortress that overlooked Cuzco. The place was called Sacsayhuaman. Pizarro decided the only way to end the siege was to take Sacsayhuaman. The Spanish force he sent there included his three brothers. Using four ladders, the Spaniards scaled the fortress walls. During the fierce battle, Juan Pizarro was killed.

Both sides fought ferociously. But once again, the Spaniards had the advantage of superior weaponry. They managed to get inside the stone fortress. Hernando Pizarro tried to take the Incas' captain captive. Before he could, the captain leapt from a fortress tower. He chose death over capture by the enemy.

"With his death," one Spaniard later recalled, "the remainder of the Indians gave way, so that Hernando Pizarro and his men were able to enter.

Manco Inca organized his army from a stone fortress, Sacsayhuaman, during his siege of Cuzco. This view shows the stone ruins of the Inca fortress.

They put all those inside the fortress to the sword—there were 1,500 of them."[6] The victory marked a turning point. Even with their small numbers, the Spaniards were now sure they could win and end the rebellion.

Even so, the Incas kept their hold on Cuzco for many months. They also set upon Lima. Francisco Pizarro sent out urgent messages to Spanish authorities for help. He promised to reward any relief expeditions with gold from his own pocket. In response, four relief parties arrived in Peru. Inca rebels slaughtered them all.[7]

Like Pizarro, Manco Inca was having trouble with his men. Since the defeat at Sacsayhuaman, many of his warriors had given up the cause. Also, Manco Inca's army was low on supplies. Some warriors deserted. They returned to their communities to sow their fields.

BACK FROM CHILE

But Manco Inca was about to face something even worse. Almagro's army returned from Chile in April 1537. The expedition had been a disaster. Indians had attacked Almagro's men. Many suffered from frostbite. All were thirsty and hungry. For all their trials, they came back with little. In Chile, Almagro had found nothing like the riches of Cuzco.

THE
DISCOVERIE AND CONQVEST
of the Prouinces of *PERV*, and
the *Nauigation in the South*
Sea, along that Coaſt.
And alſo of the ritche Mines
of *POTOSI*.

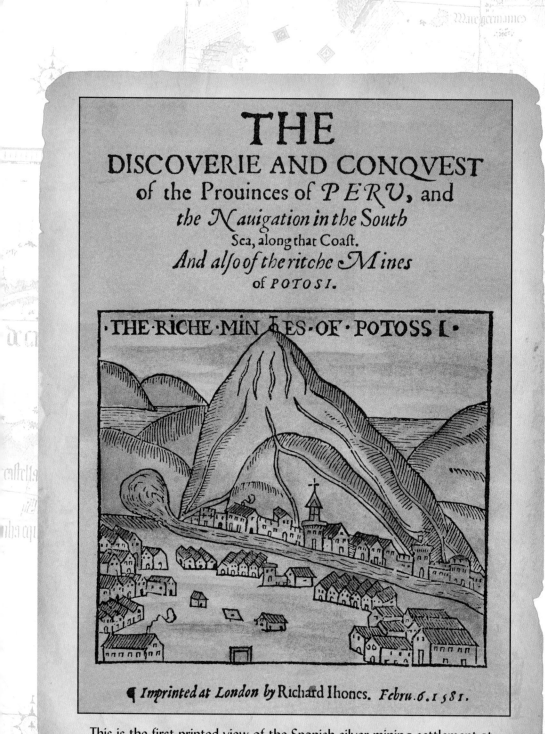

·THE·RICHE·MINᴸES·OF·POTOSSI·

❡ *Imprinted at* **London** *by* Richard Ihones. *Febru.6.1581.*

This is the first printed view of the Spanish silver mining settlement at
Potosí in 1581. Almagro failed to discover this prosperous spot on
his expedition to Chile.

Ironically, Almagro had failed to discover the greatest treasure in his realm. It was the silver deposits at Potosí in present-day Bolivia. Eight years later, the Spanish would discover Potosí. It would prove to be one of the biggest silver mines in the world.

When Almagro's men returned, they were disheveled and dispirited. But they still posed a threat to Manco Inca's dwindling army. Manco Inca decided not to fight Almagro. Instead, his forces retreated from Cuzco. They took refuge in the sacred Ollantaytambo Valley.

Almagro tried to negotiate a formal peace with Manco Inca. If he gained Manco Inca's allegiance, Almagro finally might be able to take on Pizarro. But the Inca leader refused his offer.

Hernando Pizarro had no interest in making deals with Manco Inca. He was determined to destroy the Inca force. With seventy horsemen, he rode into Ollantaytambo. The Spaniards engaged the Inca army in a bloody battle. The Incas fought with stolen Spanish weapons. As a result, they killed many Spaniards. Hernando admitted defeat and retreated to Cuzco.

Manco Inca had triumphed. But he was not sure he could win another battle with the Spanish. He remained in the Ollantaytambo valley for two more years before deciding to retreat again. His people fled into the rugged mountain forests.

There, Manco Inca and his men founded a town called Vilcabamba. This remote hideout was very difficult to reach. Manco Inca hoped the Pizarros would not dare to follow him there.

A SPANISH CIVIL WAR

While dealing with Manco Inca's rebels, Pizarro faced still another threat to his authority. Almagro remained determined to take over Cuzco. In early 1537, he made his move. Under the dark of night, his men staged an attack. They screamed, "Death to the traitors" as they stormed into Cuzco.[8] They found the building where Hernando and Gonzalo Pizarro were sleeping. When the men refused to come out, Almagro's men set it ablaze. As the Pizarros ran out, they took them captive. They placed the two brothers in chains. The other Spaniards at Cuzco surrendered. Finally, Almagro had taken possession of the old Inca capital.

Still in Lima, Francisco Pizarro knew nothing about the attack. But he had sent an army led by Alonso de Alvarado to

Diego de Almagro's army prepares for its attack on Cuzco in this 1554 engraving. This battle incited a Spanish civil war in Peru.

Cuzco. Alvarado's men were supposed to help battle Manco Inca. Instead, they found themselves fighting Almagro's army. Almagro's men won the battle. They took Alvarado captive.

The Spanish in Peru were now engaged in a full-on civil war. The Spanish king was not pleased.

He sent officials to try to make peace between Almagro and Pizarro. Almagro was willing to talk. He even agreed to release Hernando. (Gonzalo and Alvarado had escaped by bribing a guard.)

Pizarro and Almagro met at the village of Mala. Almagro tried to hug Pizarro. But Pizarro did not want his enemy to touch him. He demanded to know why Almagro thought he could take Cuzco and imprison his brothers. While they spoke, Gonzalo was hiding nearby with hundreds of men. He waited for a signal from his brother. A soldier in Almagro's army caught on to the plot. On horseback, he rushed toward the men. He convinced Almagro to ride away quickly before Gonzalo could attack.

THE END OF ALMAGRO

At sunrise on April 26, 1538, the two Spanish forces met in battle. In the gruesome fight, about 150 Spaniards were killed. Pizarro's forces, led by Hernando, were victorious. They managed to capture Almagro. They escorted their prisoner in chains back to Cuzco.

For three months, Hernando Pizarro held Almagro captive. He kept Almagro in the same cell where he had been imprisoned. Almagro begged for his life. He was an old man, he said. He had served Spain well, he insisted. But no matter what he said, Hernando refused to show him mercy.

On July 8, he ordered Almagro's execution. When Almagro was dead, Hernando's men cut off his head and placed it on a lance. Then they paraded it through Cuzco's square. Francisco Pizarro later claimed he did not order the execution. But few believed him.[9]

THE KING'S RESPONSE

King Carlos I was very upset by what happened to Almagro. He said Hernando Pizarro had no right to kill him. After all, Almagro was an official appointed by the king. By murdering Almagro, Hernando had challenged the king's authority.

Hernando decided to go to Spain. He wanted to defend his actions in person. Carlos, however, was not interested in what he had to say. The Spanish government arrested Hernando and put him in jail.

The king was also unhappy with Francisco Pizarro. Peru was becoming important to Spain. Every year, more ships of Spanish settlers arrived there. The king wanted Peru to be a stable Spanish colony. But Pizarro ran Peru as though it were his own private empire. He ignored Spanish laws and acted however he pleased.

The king also suspected Pizarro was corrupt. He was supposed to give a share of his treasures to the Crown. But Pizarro probably lied about the riches he had found. He likely underestimated his wealth in official reports. That way, he could keep part of the king's share for himself.

Spanish soldiers fueled the king's suspicions. Those returning to Spain from Peru often spoke poorly of Pizarro. He was a tyrant, they said. He was cruel to everyone, friend and foe. Especially vocal were the Almagrists. They were supporters of Almagro. Not surprisingly, they despised Pizarro for what he had done to their leader.

WARNING PIZARRO

Still in Peru, there were a handful of Almagrists. Almagro's twenty-four-year-old son, also named Diego de Almagro, led this group. These Almagrists remained furious about Almagro's execution. They were also mad that they had not received a share of Peru's gold. As a result, they were very poor.

At the time, a Spanish gentleman always wore a cape when he left his house. It was said that the Almagrists could only afford one cape between them. Because of this, only one Almagrist could appear in public at a time.

Hernando Pizarro had been worried about the Almagrists. Before he left for Spain, he gave his brother a stern warning. He told Francisco to keep his distance from the Almagrists. Hernando said, "[T]hey will kill you . . . and nothing will be left of your memory."[10]

Francisco Pizarro tried to calm the situation. He offered encomiendas to some of Almagro's friends. But they refused to take them.

Pizarro heard rumors that they were gathering weapons. He met with an Almagrist named Juan de Herrada in his orchard in Lima. He asked Herrada if the rumors were true. Herrada assured him they were not. Pizarro was relieved. He offered his guest a bunch of fresh oranges. Herrada graciously kissed Pizarro's hand before leaving.

THE DEATH OF A CONQUISTADOR

Pizarro was in his Lima palace on June 26, 1541. He was enjoying a quiet Sunday morning, talking with Martín de Alcántara in his upstairs chamber. (Alcántara was his half brother on his mother's side.) Two guests, lieutenants in Pizarro's army, waited for him downstairs.

Suddenly, a crowd of men stormed into the house. They were waving swords and knives. All were shouting, calling for Pizarro's death. Pizarro ordered his lieutenants to bar the door of the main hall. But the screaming assassins pushed in. They stabbed one lieutenant. The other lieutenant jumped out the window to escape the mob.

Pizarro hurriedly armed himself as the men ran upstairs. He fought them off with a sword and shield. He killed one man before the mob set on Alcántara. After murdering Alcántara, the killers

The execution of Francisco Pizarro.

A drawing of the death of Francisco Pizarro. He was murdered on June 26, 1541.

struck Pizarro. They stabbed him until he was too weak to raise his sword.

According to one of his murderers, Pizarro put his fingers over his mouth. They formed the sign of the cross. With his final breath, Pizarro begged to be allowed to confess his sins. His assailant, instead, grabbed a water pitcher and smashed him in the mouth. As Pizarro lay dying, the man yelled, "In Hell! You will have to confess in Hell!"[11] Those words were the last heard by the conquistador.

Chapter 6

AFTER PIZARRO

After Pizarro's brutal murder, Peru fell into chaos. The young Diego de Almagro (Almagro's son) declared himself ruler. His people plundered Lima for gold and weapons. Hernando Pizarro was still in jail. Gonzalo Pizarro was on an expedition to the Amazon region to the east. He had gone in search of a fabled land of cinnamon—a spice the Spanish valued. As a result, there were no Pizarros in Peru to challenge Almagro.

Some Spaniards were happy to support Almagro. They had been mistreated under Francisco Pizarro's rule. They were pleased that the Almagrists had killed him. Others were suspicious of Diego de Almagro. After all, Carlos I did not approve of his actions. They may not have liked Pizarro. But they were not eager to anger the king by embracing Pizarro's murderer.

THE NEW LAWS

Carlos I did not appreciate Almagro's power grab. He sent Vaca de Castro to take control of Peru. Castro's army met Almagro and his men in Cuzco. They fought, and Castro was the victor. He had Almagro executed in the town square.

The king was pleased with this turn of events. He was glad to get rid of Almagro, who had rebelled against his authority. He was also happy to see the end of Francisco Pizarro's rule. For too long, he had commanded Peru with no regard for the king's wishes.

In 1544, the king sent Blasco Núñez Vela to take Castro's place. The king gave him the title viceroy of Peru. Núñez Vela strictly enforced what were called the New Laws. These laws limited the powers of the conquistadores.

The New Laws also called for the end of American Indian slavery in Peru. For years, the Spanish court had debated whether Indians were human or not. The Spanish finally decided they were. Spain therefore felt obligated to grant Indians at least some basic rights.

GONZALO PIZARRO'S CHALLENGE

The encomenderos were furious over the New Laws. These laws threatened their privileged lives on their encomiendas.

Gonzalo Pizarro was especially angry. He would not obey the New Laws, even if it meant going to war with the king's appointed viceroy. Gonzalo assembled an army to attack Núñez Vela and his supporters. On January 18, 1546, Gonzalo's men defeated the enemy force and killed Núñez Vela.

Gonzalo Pizarro then declared himself the rightful ruler of Peru.

The king, of course, did not see it that way. He sent Pedro de la Gasca to take back control. Pizarro had about five hundred men. Gasca's army was twice as large. Even so, Pizarro managed to defeat the larger force in October 1547.

Gasca learned a lesson. He skillfully courted the support of the Spaniards in Peru. Many distrusted Pizarro. Gasca was able to convince them to join his side. The next time Gasca battled with Gonzalo Pizarro, Gasca had two thousand soldiers. On April 9, 1548, his army finally defeated Gonzalo Pizarro's force. Pizarro surrendered. Gasca executed him and forty-eight other rebel leaders. Gonzalo Pizarro's death put an end to the Spanish civil wars in Peru.

THE FATE OF HERNANDO PIZARRO

Hernando, the last surviving Pizarro brother, fared better. When Francisco and Gonzalo were killed, he was still in prison in Spain. Hernando's imprisonment was fairly comfortable. He received decent treatment. Hernando was even allowed to have servants wait on him. He was also permitted to manage the family's wealth from his prison cell. Because of this, he remained a rich man.

While in prison, Hernando got married. His bride was Francisca, the daughter of his brother Francisco. Francisca was supposed to inherit riches from her father. But Hernando offered to give this fortune to the king. In return, the king granted him his freedom in 1561.

Hernando then moved back to Trujillo. He was one of the richest men in Spain. He built a great palace in his hometown. There, Hernando Pizarro lived a long, contented life. Unlike his brothers, he died a natural death in 1578.

Gonzalo Pizarro being led to his execution. With his death, the civil wars in Peru ended.

THE INCA OF VILCABAMBA

The Inca rebels at Vilcabamba were very pleased when they heard about Francisco Pizarro's death. In fact, their leader Manco Inca tried to help the Almagrists. He wanted to reward them for killing Pizarro. Manco Inca offered to hide some of them in the jungle.

It was a fatal misjudgment. The Almagrists were trying to find a way to get back into the king's good graces. They knew Manco Inca's rebels had long been a source of anxiety to the Crown. The Almagrists decided the king and his viceroy might pardon them for murdering Pizarro if they killed Manco Inca.

While playing a game of horseshoes with Manco Inca, they struck. Seven Almagrists stabbed him over and over from behind. His nine-year-old son, Titu Cusi, witnessed the scene. When the boy tried to help his bloodied father, his assailants almost killed him with a lance. After three days of pain, Manco Inca died.

Manco Inca's son Sayri Túpac then took over Vilcabamba. After his death, his two brothers—Titu Cusi and Túpac Amaru—led the rebels. They were few in number. But they remained a thorn in the side of Spanish officials.

In 1571, Francisco de Toledo became the new viceroy. He decided to destroy the rebel stronghold at Vilcabamba. He sent a force of 250 soldiers into the mountain town. Túpac Amaru tried to flee, but he was captured.

The soldiers brought Túpac Amaru to Cuzco. Spaniards crammed into the square to watch his execution. Túpac Amaru addressed the crowd. He calmly said that he accepted his fate. An executioner then killed him. The last organized Inca resistance to Spanish rule was over.

A Dwindling Population

Toledo was a good administrator.[1] Under his rule, Peru was fairly peaceful. He was also interested in Inca history. He had his men interview Incas about their people's past. They also spoke to Pizarro's original band of conquistadores. These records provide historians with much of what is known about the Incas and the conquest of Peru.

In the late 1500s, the Incas were no longer slaves. But the Spanish still mistreated them. The Incas had to give gifts of goods and services to the king. For many, this meant working at the great silver mine at Potosí. The Spanish extracted silver there for almost one hundred years. For a time, it was the largest city in the Americas.

Every year, thousands of Incas labored in the mines. The work was very difficult. They were exhausted, forced to work day and night. Many Incas died mining silver. Others died of starvation. The old Incas had kept food stores. In times of famine, they could tap these stores to keep their people fed. The Inca people also built irrigation canals to water fields. This way, they could grow enough extra food to survive lean years. The Spanish, however, abandoned these practices. They were too focused on finding riches. As a result, if a year's harvest was bad, many Incas had nothing to eat.

The Incas still suffered and died from European diseases. Over time, the epidemics took a severe toll. The Indian population fell swiftly. Within one hundred years after Pizarro's arrival, it dropped from about twelve million to less than one million people. So many Incas died that the Spanish imported African slaves as workers.

SPANISH INFLUENCES

After the Spanish conquest, the Incas lost their way of life. They were compelled to adopt Spanish customs. The Spanish especially wanted to wipe out the Inca's religion. If Incas practiced it, Spaniards punished them harshly. They insisted the Incas embrace Catholicism. Today, most people of Indian ancestry in modern-day Peru are Catholics.

The Spanish also brought their language to South America. In time, it became the language spoken by most people in the lands of the old Inca Empire. However, millions of people in Peru still speak an Inca language called Quechua.

Because of Pizarro's invasion, the population of Peru has also changed. Spaniards and Indians began to marry one another. Today, more than two-thirds of Peruvians are mestizos—people of mixed Spanish and Indian ancestry.

INCA WAYS SURVIVE

The influence of the Spanish conquistadores is still felt in Peru. But that country is no longer under Spanish control. Peru gained its independence from Spain in 1824.

However, the economy set up by the Spanish still affects modern Peruvians. Pizarro established the encomienda system there. It allowed a few Spaniards to live well off the labor of many Incas. Today, the majority of Peruvians are very poor. A small, elite group continues to hold most of the country's wealth.

Despite these influences, some aspects of traditional Inca life have survived. Some Peruvians enjoy Inca food and drink. They eat *chuno* (dried potato) and drink *chicha* (corn beer). Artists have also preserved Inca crafts. Contemporary metalworkers, pottery makers, and weavers all draw inspiration from the artifacts left behind by the ancient Incas.

The Incas' world also survives in ruins of their old cities. The most famous is Machu Picchu. The ninth Inca, Pachacuti, built it in about 1450. High up in the Andes Mountains, this city was forgotten for centuries. A young American scholar named Hiram Bingham rediscovered it in 1911. Since then, many thousands of people have come to Peru each year just to see its amazing buildings.

PIZARRO REEXAMINED

In 1977, workmen made another surprising discovery. In an old cathedral in Lima, they found a metal box. Inside was part of a sword and a pair of silver spurs. It also contained several bones and a human skull. A message was inscribed on the box. It read: "This is the head of the Lord Marques Don Francisco Pizarro who discovered and conquered these realms of Peru."[2]

Pizarro's remains may have been long forgotten. But his role in history was not. Since his death, many historians have examined his life. Some have praised Pizarro for his courage. But most have condemned him for his brutality and greed.

He has been especially criticized for his betrayal of Atahualpa. By many accounts, he admired the Incas' great leader. But in the end, Pizarro ordered the execution of Atahualpa to ensure his control over Peru.

People in both Spain and Peru also still debate Pizarro's legacy. In his hometown of Trujillo, Spain, for instance, he is celebrated with a large statue in the town square. In Lima, Peru, however, Pizarro is viewed less favorably. A statue of him once stood near the city center. It offended many Peruvians. For years, they protested against honoring the man who had killed so many of their Inca ancestors. Because of their demands, the city moved the statue in 2003.

THE LEGACY OF CONQUEST

Pizarro may have been despicable. But he did not try to pretend he was motivated by anything but the basest of instincts. Once a priest asked him to try to convert the Incas to Christianity. Pizarro bluntly dismissed the priest's suggestion. "I did not come here for those reasons," he told the priest. "I came here to take away their gold."[3]

Not all conquistadores had such a lack of guilt. In 1590, Mansio Serra de Leguizamón was dying. He was the last surviving member of Pizarro's invading army.

Leguizamón dictated his will. In it, he directly addressed the Spanish king, then Philip II. Leguizamón told the king that the Incas had been a great and noble people. They feared, but also respected, their powerful leaders. In the Inca world, he said, "all things, from the greatest to the smallest, had their place and order."[4]

After the Spanish conquest, though, the Incas began to change. Leguizamón said the Spaniards' "bad example" had unleashed greed and evil into their world. He said this was "something which much touch Your Majesty's conscience as it does mine." It was also "something that requires to be remedied."[5]

Leguizamón was an old man with a very guilty conscience. No doubt if he could have undone the wrongs he had committed as a young man, he would have wanted to. But that was impossible.

An American scholar, Hiram Bingham, rediscovered the ruins of Machu Picchu in 1911. The remarkable ancient site is visited by thousands of people each year.

Downtown Lima, Peru. Many Peruvians do not view Pizarro with great admiration.

Nothing could erase the effects of the momentous events he participated in.

In 1532, Francisco Pizarro and his motley followers had boldly attacked thousands of Incas at Cajamarca. And amazingly, they had won the battle. That one moment in time had forever changed the course of history.

Chapter Notes

Chapter 1. A Line in the Sand

1. John Hemming, "Pizarro: Conqueror of the Inca," *National Geographic,* vol. 181, no. 4, February 1992, p. 98.

2. Michael Wood, *Conquistadors* (Berkeley, Calif.: University of California Press, 2000), p. 112.

Chapter 2. A Soldier of Fortune

1. John Hemming, "Pizarro: Conqueror of the Inca," *National Geographic,* vol. 181, no. 4, February 1992, pp. 98–99.

2. Ibid., p. 99.

3. Rafael Varón Gabai, *Francisco Pizarro and His Brothers: The Illusion of Power in Sixteenth-Century Peru* (Norman, Okla.: University of Oklahoma Press, 1997), p. 11.

4. Stuart Stirling, *Pizarro: Conqueror of the Inca* (Stroud, Gloucestershire: Sutton Publishing, 2005), p. 3.

5. Pedro Pizarro, *Relation of the Discovery and Conquest of the Kingdom of Peru,* vol. 1 (New York: Kraus Reprint Co., 1969), p. 144.

6. Stirling, p. 17.

7. Ibid.

Chapter 3. The Conquistador and the Inca

1. John Hemming, "Pizarro: Conqueror of the Inca," *National Geographic,* vol. 181, no. 4, February 1992, p. 112.

2. Stuart Stirling, *Pizarro: Conqueror of the Inca* (Stroud, Gloucestershire: Sutton Publishing, 2005), p. 32.

3. Michael Wood, *Conquistadors* (Berkeley, Calif.: University of California Press, 2000), p. 129.

4. John Hemming, *The Conquest of the Incas* (New York: Harcourt, Brace, Jovanovich, 1970), p. 32.

5. Stirling, p. 38.

6. Ibid., p. 41.

7. William H. Prescott, *History of the Conquest of Peru,* vol. 1, reprint (New York: Barnes & Noble World Digital Library, 2003), p. 430.

8. Hemming, *National Geographic,* p. 104.

9. Wood, p. 134.

10. Prescott, p. 458.

11. Stirling, p. 136.

Chapter 4. Exploiting the Incas

1. John Hemming, "Pizarro: Conqueror of the Inca," *National Geographic,* vol. 181, no. 4, February 1992, p. 110.

2. Stuart Stirling, *Pizarro: Conqueror of the Inca* (Stroud, Gloucestershire: Sutton Publishing, 2005), p. 44.

3. Michael Wood, *Conquistadors* (Berkeley, Calif.: University of California Press, 2000), p. 143.

4. Ibid.

5. Stirling, pp. 45–46.

6. Ibid., p. 47.

7. Ibid., p. 48.

8. Ibid., p. 49.

9. Ibid., pp. 54–55.

10. William H. Prescott, *History of the Conquest of Peru,* vol. 1, reprint (New York: Barnes & Noble World Digital Library, 2003), p. 524.

11. Ibid., p. 45.

12. Hemming, *National Geographic,* p. 111.

13. Stirling, p. 62.

14. Hemming, *National Geographic,* p. 111.

15. Wood, p. 148.

Chapter 5. Spaniard Against Spaniard

1. Stuart Stirling, *Pizarro: Conqueror of the Inca* (Stroud, Gloucestershire: Sutton Publishing, 2005), p. 87.

2. Ibid., p. 93.

3. Ibid.

4. Michael Wood, *Conquistadors* (Berkeley, Calif.: University of California Press, 2000), p. 160.

5. Titu Cusi Yupanqui, *An Inca Account of the Conquest of Peru* (Boulder, Colo.: University Press of Colorado, 2005), p. 88.

6. John Hemming, *The Conquest of the Incas* (New York: Harcourt, Brace, Jovanovich, 1970), p. 201.

7. Stirling, p. 102.

8. Ibid., p. 107.

9. Ibid., p. 115.

10. Ibid., p. 121.

11. John Hemming, "Pizarro: Conqueror of the Inca," *National Geographic,* vol. 181, no. 4, February 1992, p. 102.

Chapter 6. After Pizarro

1. Stuart Stirling, *Pizarro: Conqueror of the Inca* (Stroud, Gloucestershire: Sutton Publishing, 2005), p. 200.

2. Ibid., p. v.

3. Ibid., p. 211.

4. Ibid., p. 213.

5. Ibid., p. 214.

Glossary

booty—Goods and treasures seized from an enemy in wartime.

chicha—An Inca beer made from corn.

colony—A region ruled by a government in another land.

conquest—The takeover of a region by force.

conquistador—A sixteenth-century Spanish soldier charged with conquering peoples in North and South America.

empire—Large territory governed by a single ruler.

encomienda—A grant to a Spaniard of the fruits of Indian labor on a specific tract of land.

epidemic—The widespread outbreak of disease.

hidalgo—Spanish title bestowed on military leaders.

immunity—The human body's natural defenses against disease.

Inca—A ruler of the Inca Empire.

Incas—Indian people who lived in an empire that stretched from Ecuador to Chile during the early sixteenth century.

ingot—A solid block of metal.

litter—A platform held aloft of the shoulders of two or more people, designed to carry a distinguished person.

llama—South American mammal used as a pack animal and as a source of wool and meat.

mestizo—A person of mixed Spanish and Indian ancestry.

mutiny—A rebellion of soldiers or sailors against their commander.

noble—Person of high social rank.

plaza—An open area in a town or city used for gatherings and ceremonies.

siege—Long-term military assault on a town, city, or fort.

smallpox—A highly infectious disease that, before the late twentieth century, often resulted in death.

viceroy—A government's representative appointed to rule a colony.

Further Reading

Books

Bingham, Jane. *The Inca Empire*. Chicago: Raintree, 2007.

Gruber, Beth. *National Geographic Investigates Ancient Inca: Archaeology Unlocks the Secrets of the Inca's Past*. Washington, D.C.: National Geographic Children's Books, 2007.

Ingram, Scott. *Francisco Pizarro*. San Diego, Calif.: Blackbirch Press, 2002.

Meltzer, Milton. *Francisco Pizarro: The Conquest of Peru*. New York: Benchmark Books, 2005.

Mountjoy, Shane. *Francisco Pizarro and the Conquest of the Inca*. Philadelphia: Chelsea House Publishers, 2006.

Somervill, Barbara A. *Francisco Pizarro: Conqueror of the Incas*. Minneapolis, Minn.: Compass Point Books, 2005.

Internet Addresses

The Inca—All Empires
<http://www.allempires.com/article/index.php?q=inca#section_1>

PBS: Conquistadors—Pizarro
<http://www.pbs.org/conquistadors/pizarro/pizarro_flat.html>

Index